DATE DUE

FOLLETT

What Do You Call a Group of Butterflies?
And Other Insect Groups

EMMA NATHAN

BLACKBIRCH PRESS, INC.
WOODBRIDGE, CONNECTICUT

Published by Blackbirch Press, Inc.
260 Amity Road
Woodbridge, CT 06525
web site: http://www.blackbirch.com
e-mail: staff@blackbirch.com

© 2000 Blackbirch Press, Inc.
First Edition

Printed in Singapore

10 9 8 7 6 5 4 3 2 1

Photo Credits
Cover, pages 3, 5, 7, 9: ©PhotoSpin, Inc; pages 4, 8, 12, 22: ©Corel Corporation; page 6: ©Fritz Polkino/Peter Arnold, Inc.; page 10: ©Nuridsany et Pérennou/Photo Researchers, Inc.; page 11: ©Manfred Kage/Peter Arnold, Inc.; pages 13, 15, 17, 19: ©Artville LLC; page 14: ©Patti Murray/Animals Animals; pages 16, 20: ©Hans Pfletschinger/Peter Arnold, Inc.; page 18: ©Gianni Tortoli/Photo Researchers, Inc.; page 21: ©Norm Thomas/Photo Researchers, Inc.

Library of Congress Cataloging-in-Publication Data
Nathan, Emma.
    What do you call a group of butterflies? : and other insect groups / by Emma Nathan.
    p. cm. — (What do you call a —)
Includes index.
Summary: Explains the terms used for groups of insects, including ants, termites, flies, and grasshoppers and provides information on the group behavior of these creatures.
    ISBN 1-56711-359-1 (hardcover : alk. paper)
    1. Insects—Miscellanea—Juvenile literature. 2. English language—Collective nouns—Juvenile literature. [1. Insects—Miscellanea. 2. English language—Collective nouns. 3. Questions and answers.] I. Title.
QL467.2.N29 2000   00-008229
595.7—dc21   CIP

Contents

What do you call a group of ants?

Ants That Advance

Ants are probably the most social of all insects. No matter what the species, ants will always live with other ants in colonies. The size of a colony can range from 10 ants up to 1 million! No matter what the size, each colony is organized the same way. Each has 1 queen, whose only job is to lay eggs. All the other females in the colony are worker ants— they find food, raise the young, and maintain and defend the nest. Male ants die soon after mating with the queen, which is their only function.

A group of ants is called a colony.

What do you call group of bees**?**

Un Bee-lievable

Most bees prefer to live alone. Honeybees and bumble-bees, however, are 2 species of social bees. They live and work in huge colonies or hives. Most of the bees in a grist or hive are female workers. The males, called drones, mate with the queen and then die. The queen is the one that lays and cares for the first batch of eggs, which starts a colony. After that, her female offspring take over the duties of running the hive. Eventually, there may be between 300 to 400 bees in 1 hive.

A group of bees is called a hive or a grist.

What do you call a group of butterflies?

It's Great to Migrate

There are more than 90,000 species of butterfly, which makes them the second most common insect on the planet after beetles. Monarch butterflies gather into large armies before migrating south for winter. These migrations are some of the longest journeys taken by any animal. Sometimes, millions of migrating butterflies will form huge clouds. One army in Argentina measured 600 feet (200 meters) high, a mile wide, and several miles long!

A group of butterflies is called an army.

What do you call a group of flies?

Pesky Business

Flies are everywhere. They live in almost every kind of habitat on Earth. Some species can produce up to 250 eggs at one time. In an average lifetime, certain female flies will produce more than 1,000 offspring. Flies need to reproduce quickly and in great numbers. That's because most of them don't live very long. Depending on the species, a fly will live anywhere from a few hours to more than a month.

A group of flies is called a business.

What do you call a group of gnats?

All Gnat-ural

To humans, gnats are tiny, hard-to-see pests. Not all gnats bite, but they are a nuisance—especially when they swarm together in large numbers. Wet, marshy areas and piles of rotting matter attract these insects. Gnats lay their eggs in water, which is why they are most often seen at ponds, lakes, or at the edges of streams—especially in summer. Some gnats are so small that they can slip through human clothing. If they bite, they produce an irritating itch.

A group of gnats is called a cloud or a horde.

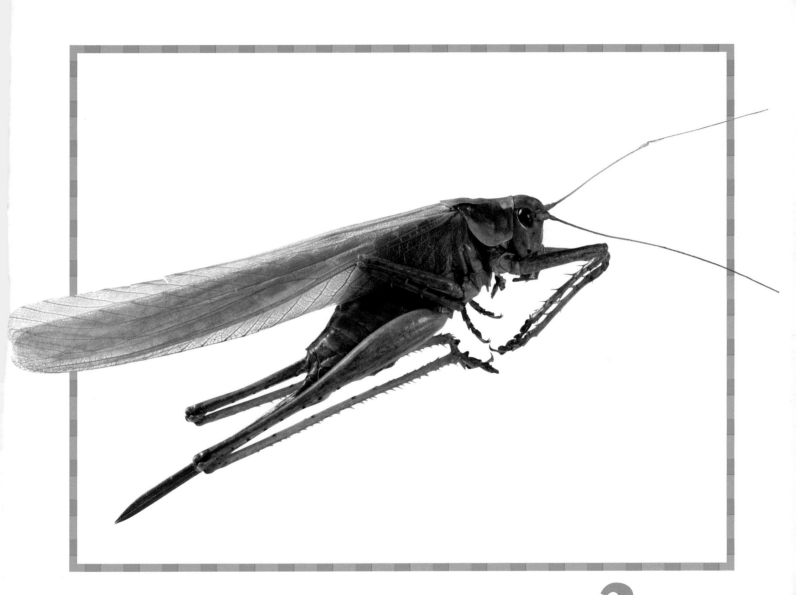

What do you call a group of grasshoppers?

13

Muster the Cluster

With their relatively long, springy legs, grasshoppers are some of the best jumpers in the insect world. On average, a grasshopper can leap more than 20 times the length of its body—that's like you jumping 80 to 100 feet (33 meters) at once! During the dry season, grasshoppers will gather and migrate to better food sources. Often, they mass together at night and fly on wind currents—soaring at altitudes up to 3,300 feet (1,000 meters)!

A group of grasshoppers is called a cluster.

What do you call a group of hornets?

WHAT DO YOU KNOW?

Dressed to Nest

Hornets are social wasps that form cooperative colonies. To begin a nest, a female chews plant or wood material, mixing it with her saliva to make paper. She then creates a series of connected paper cells and lays an egg in each one. When the eggs hatch into larvae, they are fed bits of chewed-up insects. When the young have matured, they begin building more cells for the nest so the colony can grow.

A group of hornets is called a nest.

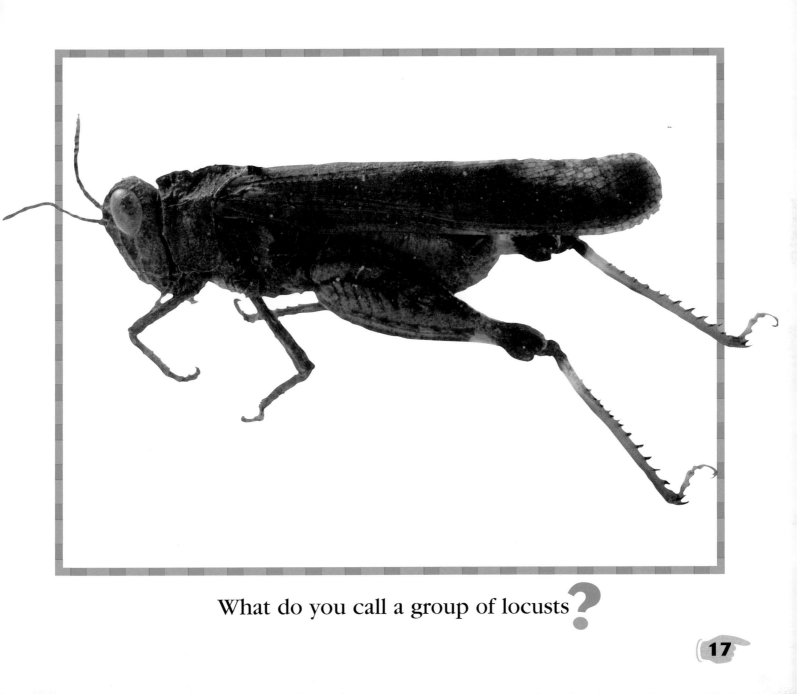

What do you call a group of locusts?

Focused on the Locust

Locust is really another name for a short-horned grasshopper. These insects like to gather in large groups, especially when they're on the move. The largest single plague of locusts ever recorded was in Africa, when more than 1 billion insects swarmed into Kenya. It was estimated that this plague covered 77 square miles (200 sq. kilometers)! Locusts are also long-distance champions. Some types have been known to travel 3,000 miles (4,500 kilometers), often crossing open oceans.

A group of locusts is called a plague.

What do you call a group of robber flies ?

Swarm and Cozy

Robber flies have excellent vision and sharp mouthparts. Swarms of these insects can be found patrolling fields and prairies, looking for prey. Once a robber fly finds a wasp, bee, or other insect, it is able to catch its prey in midair and paralyze it. The fly then pierces its victim's skin and uses its long proboscis (tubelike structure) to suck out the blood.

A group of robber flies is called a swarm.

What do you call a group of termites **?**

Termite Delight

Termites, like ants, are quite organized when it comes to living together. Each colony has 3 classes of termite: royal pair (king and queen), workers, and soldiers who protect the nest. A termite colony begins with a king and queen, who prepare the first nest and mate. Once their offspring are old enough, the new workers begin to care for the nest and the next batch of eggs. In just a short time, there can be more than 1 million members in a single mound!

A group of termites is called a colony.

Glossary

Altitude—the height of something.

Cooperative—working together to reach a goal.

Current—movement of air; wind.

Drones—male bees in a hive.

Habitat—the place and natural conditions in a which an animal or plant lives.

Migrate—to travel for a certain amount of time during a season or stage in an animal's life.

Nuisance—something that bothers you.

Proboscis— long, tubelike structure that some animals have to suck up fluids.

Reproduce—to mate and produce young.

Social—animals that live in groups instead of on their own.

Species—one of the groups into which a plant or animal is divided, according to shared characteristics.

For More Information

Books

Crewe, Sabrina. *The Bee* (Life Cycles). Chatham, NJ: Raintree/Steck Vaughn, 1997.

Lavies, Bianca. *Monarch Butterflies: Mysterious Travelers.* New York, NY: Dutton Children's Books, 1992.

Pascoe, Elaine. *Flies* (Nature Close-Up). Woodbridge, CT: Blackbirch Press, Inc., 2000.

Perry, Phyllis Jean. *The Fiddlehoppers: Crickets, Katydids, and Locusts* (First Books). Danbury, CT: Franklin Watts, Inc., 1995.

Web Sites

Bees
Learn about the different parts of a bee's body, and also how bee species are different— www.greensmiths.com/bees.htm

The Bug Page
View the insect gallery, hear some bug sounds, and learn where different insects are found— www.thebugpage.com

Index